W9-BMZ-783

Questions and Answers: Countries

Peru

A Question and Answer Book

by Muriel L. Dubois

Consultant:
Thomas A. Brown
Professor of History
Augustana College
Rock Island, Illinois

Capstone
press

Mankato, Minnesota

Fact Finders is published by Capstone Press,
151 Good Counsel Drive, P.O. Box 669, Mankato, Minnesota 56002.
www.capstonepress.com

Library of Congress Cataloging-in-Publication Data
Dubois, Muriel L.
    Peru: a question and answer book / by Muriel L. Dubois.
    p. cm.—(Fact finders. Questions and answers. Countries)
    Includes bibliographical references and index.
    ISBN 0-7368-3758-2 (hardcover)
    ISBN 0-7368-5207-7 (paperback)
    1. Peru—Juvenile literature. I. Title. II. Series.
F3408.5.D83 2005
985—dc22
                                                               2004009813

Summary: Describes the geography, history, economy, and culture of Peru in a
    question-and-answer format.

Editorial Credits
Donald Lemke, editor; Kia Adams, set designer; Kate Opseth, book designer; Nancy Steers,
    map illustrator; Wanda Winch, photo researcher; Scott Thoms, photo editor

Photo Credits
Art Directors/Chris Rennie, 25; Art Directors/M. Barlow, 4; Corbis/Reuters, 9;
Corbis/Reuters/Rickey Rogers, 18–19; Corbis Royalty-Free, 1; Cory Langley, 17; Getty
Images/Hulton Archive, 6; James P. Rowan, 21; Nature Picture Library/Pete Oxford, 12;
Pete & Jill Yearneau, 29 (bill and coins); Photodisc/Sexto Sol/Adalberto Rios Szalay, cover
(background); South American Pictures, 7; South American Pictures/Tony Morrison, 11, 13,
14–15, 23, 27; StockHaus Ltd., 29 (flag); Victor Englebert, cover (foreground)

Artistic Effects
Photodisc/Don Tremain, 18; Photodisc/GK Hart/Vikki Hart, 24

1 2 3 4 5 6 10 09 08 07 06 05

Table of Contents

Features

Where is Peru?

Peru is a large country on the western coast of South America. It is slightly smaller than the U.S. state of Alaska.

Peru has three types of land. The coastal desert stretches from Ecuador to Chile. It is one of the driest places on earth. The Andes Mountains border the coast. They divide the coast from an area of rain forests in the east.

The Andes Mountains surround many fertile valleys in Peru. ➤

Map of Peru

Legend

- ⊛ Capital
- ● City
- ▲ Mountain
- ⛰ Mountain Range
- ⌇ River

ECUADOR

COLOMBIA

Napo River

Amazon River

● Iquitos

Marañón River

Ucayali River

BRAZIL

Cajamarca ●

Chimbote ●

▲ Mount Huascarán

Andes Mountains

Lima ⊛

PERU

PACIFIC OCEAN

Cuzco ●

BOLIVIA

Arequipa ●

Lake Titicaca

CHILE

Scale

| 0 | 250 | 500 Miles |

| 0 | 250 | 500 Kilometers |

Peru also has many rivers and lakes. The Amazon River starts in Peru. It is the second longest river in the world. Peru shares Lake Titicaca with Bolivia. It is the highest lake in the world used by ships.

5

When did Peru become a country?

Peru became an **independent** country on July 28, 1821. Hundreds of years earlier, native **empires** controlled the area. The Inca empire ruled from about 1300 to 1535. The Inca built roads and cities such as Cuzco.

Between 1525 and 1535, Spain conquered the Inca. Spain ruled Peru for almost 300 years. The Spanish made the Inca their slaves.

In 1532, Spanish explorer Francisco Pizarro (far right) captured Atahualpa, the last Inca ruler. ➤

In the early 1800s, General José de San Martín helped free Peru from Spain.

By the late 1700s, the people of Peru started fighting against Spanish rule. Soldiers from other South American countries helped in the fight. In 1821, José de San Martín declared Peru free from Spain.

What type of government does Peru have?

Peru is a constitutional republic. Peru's government is organized much like the U.S. government. Both countries have a set of written laws called a constitution. Both also elect their leaders and have three branches of government.

Peruvians elect a president and two vice presidents to the **executive branch**. Peru's president serves a five-year term.

Fact!

In 2000, Peruvians who did not vote risked a fine.

Members of congress form the **legislative branch** of Peru's government. The 121 members write the laws of Peru.

The supreme court and other lower courts make up the **judicial branch**. They help explain the country's laws.

What kind of housing does Peru have?

In cities, Peruvians live in houses and apartments. Some rich families own large houses with gardens. Poor families often live together in shacks made of tin or cardboard. Most shacks do not have running water or bathrooms.

Where do people in Peru live?

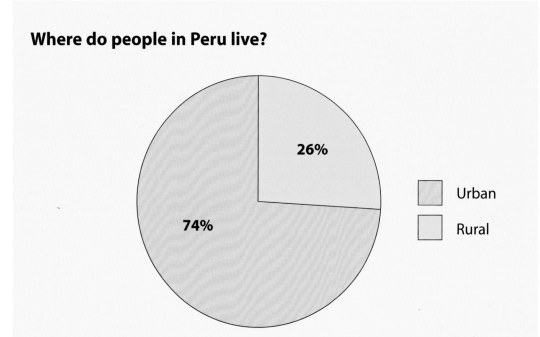

26%

74%

Urban

Rural

In the capital city of Lima, poor Peruvians often live in run-down neighborhoods called slums.

In rural areas, people often build their own homes. Uros Indians build their houses on Lake Titicaca. Their homes float on islands made of **reeds**. In the past, enemies of the Uros found it difficult to reach these floating homes.

What are Peru's forms of transportation?

Some Peruvians own cars, but most people use public transportation. In cities, they ride on large buses called *micros*. These buses can carry about 70 people. They also ride in smaller buses called *combis* and in taxis.

An Aymara Indian paddles a reed boat on Lake Titicaca. ➤

In cities, some Peruvians walk from place to place. Others travel in cars and buses.

Peru has few paved roads. During heavy rains, many roads are too muddy for travel. Instead, people fly to and from most large cities on airplanes. Some Peruvians travel by train. Others use motorboats or canoes to travel on lakes and rivers.

What are Peru's major industries?

Agriculture is a major **industry** in Peru. Farmers grow sugarcane, coffee, rice, and cotton. Peruvians **export** cotton to countries around the world. Companies use it to make shirts, sweaters, and other clothing.

Mining is another important industry. Peruvians mine copper, lead, zinc, silver, and other metals. In the past, they mined dried bird droppings, called **guano,** from coastal islands. Today, some farmers still use guano to help crops grow.

What does Peru import and export?	
Imports	*Exports*
food	copper
machinery	cotton
petroleum	fish products

Workers harvest cotton from one of Peru's many coastal farms.

People in Peru fish off the country's coast. They catch small fish called anchovies. Most anchovies are ground and dried into fish meal. Farmers feed fish meal to their cows, goats, and pigs.

What is school like in Peru?

Children begin one year of preschool when they are 5 years old. They then spend six years in grade school and two years in secondary school.

At age 14, some students go to academic secondary school. These schools prepare students for college. Other students learn job skills at technical secondary schools.

Fact!

Founded in 1551, the National Autonomous University of San Marcos in Peru is the oldest university in South America.

A teacher helps a group of Peruvian students with a class lesson.

Public school is free in Peru. Most city schools have books, gym equipment, and computers. Public schools in Peru's poorer towns often have few school supplies.

What are Peru's favorite sports and games?

Soccer is Peru's most popular sport. Some Peruvian children play soccer on local fields. Others practice on city streets. Peru's national soccer teams play in the World Cup and the Olympics. In 2004, Peru hosted a soccer tournament called Copa América. Twelve countries competed for the championship.

Women's volleyball is another favorite sport in Peru. Fans cheer for the national team at the Volleyball World Cup and other events.

Fact!

In 1988, the women's volleyball team won Peru's first Olympic medal.

Children in Peru enjoy playing soccer with friends.

People in Peru also enjoy two types of bullfighting. In Lima, fans watch a **matador** fight and kill a bull. In southern Peru, fans watch two bulls fight each other. Peruvians bet on which bull is the strongest.

What are the traditional art forms in Peru?

Weaving is one of Peru's oldest arts. Hundreds of years ago, Inca artists wove pictures of gods and animals into cloth. Today, some Peruvians still weave. They use wool from local animals, including **alpacas** and llamas.

Carving is another Peruvian art form. Some artists make religious statues from wood and stone. Other people carve designs on small dried pumpkins or gourds.

Fact!

Researchers have found cloth in Peru that is at least 4,000 years old.

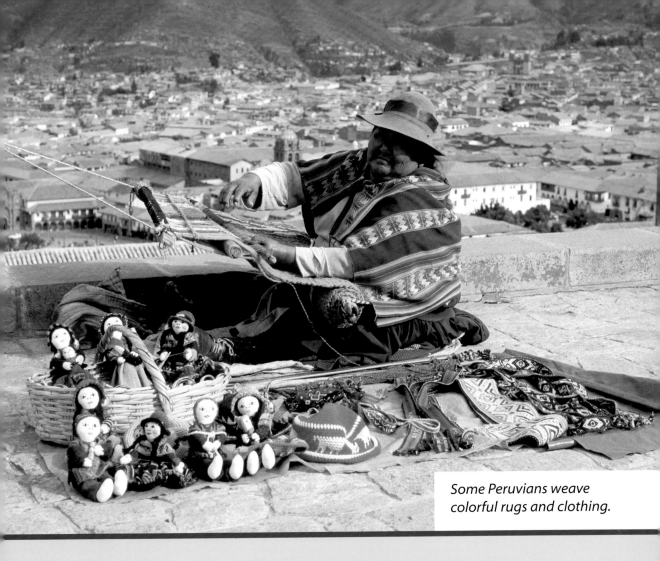

Some Peruvians weave colorful rugs and clothing.

Silversmiths and goldsmiths make pins, earrings, and necklaces. They also mold silver and gold into religious objects. These objects include crosses and cups for church services.

What major holidays do people in Peru celebrate?

Peruvians celebrate many religious festivals. In Lima, they honor a painting of Jesus Christ called the *Lord of Miracles*. It has survived earthquakes and other damaging events since 1655. Every October, people follow the image as it is carried through the streets. Many followers wear purple during the celebrations. In Peru, October is known as purple month.

What other holidays do people in Peru celebrate?

Christmas Day
Good Friday
Holy Thursday
New Year's Day

In October, thousands of Peruvians gather in Lima to honor the Lord of Miracles.

Peruvians also enjoy many national holidays. On July 28 and 29, families celebrate Peru's independence from Spain. Towns often have fairs and parades on these days. People in Peru celebrate Labor Day on May 1.

What are the traditional foods of Peru?

In cities, Peruvians eat vegetables from local markets. Corn, potatoes, and peppers are part of most meals. Peruvians use corn to make everything from flour to jelly. Red chili peppers called *ají* grow in Peru. People often spice their dishes with this hot pepper.

In the mountains, people eat meat dishes. Dried meat is called *charqui*. Peruvians make *charqui* from beef, llama, or alpaca.

Fact!

In Peru, guinea pigs aren't just cute pets. They are also raised for food. Peruvians use guinea pig meat in many dishes.

In Peru, people buy fruits and vegetables from local markets.

In Peru's coastal areas, many people enjoy fish. Fish soaked in lemon or passion fruit juice is called seviche. Most seviche recipes include oil, onion, and pepper.

What is family life like in Peru?

Many families in Peru are large. In cities, children, parents, and grandparents often share one home. Each child has godparents. This couple helps raise and protect the child. Many families also have servants to help around the house.

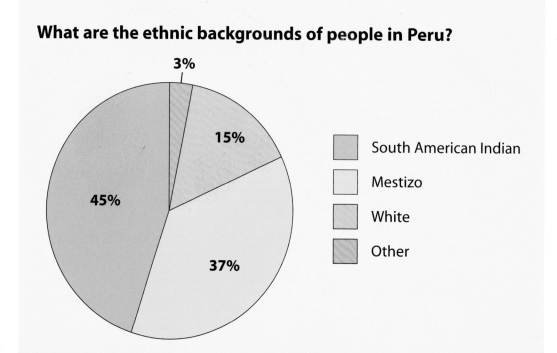

What are the ethnic backgrounds of people in Peru?

3%

15%

45%

37%

- South American Indian
- Mestizo
- White
- Other

A Peruvian family enjoys an afternoon together.

In rural areas, many families are poor.
Children help support the family. They
do farm chores. Some children work as
servants. Other children help their family
by selling bread, newspapers, or candy.

Peru Fast Facts

Official name:

Republic of Peru

Population:

27,544,305 people

Land area:

494,211 square miles
(1, 280, 000 square kilometers)

Capital city:

Lima

Average annual precipitation (Lima):

2 inches (5 centimeters)

Languages:

Spanish and Quechua

Average January temperature (Lima):

60 degrees Fahrenheit
(16 degrees Celsius)

Natural resources:

copper, gold, guano, lead, petroleum, silver, zinc

Average July temperature (Lima):

71 degrees Fahrenheit
(22 degrees Celsius)

Religions:

Roman Catholic   90%
Other   10%

Money and Flag

Money:

Peru's money is called the nuevo sol. In 2004, 1 U.S. dollar equaled 3.36 nuevos soles. One Canadian dollar equaled 2.61 nuevos soles.

Flag:

Peru's flag has three stripes. The red and white colors stand for the Inca people. Peru's coat of arms is on the white stripe. It has three pictures. They stand for the animals, vegetables, and minerals of Peru.

Learn to Speak Spanish

People in Peru speak Spanish. Learn to speak some Spanish words using the chart below.

English	Spanish	Pronunciation
hello	hola	(OH-lah)
good morning	buenos días	(BWAY-nohs DEE-ahs)
good-bye	adiós	(ah-dee-OHS)
please	por favor	(POR fah-VOR)
thank you	gracias	(GRAH-see-us)
yes	sí	(SEE)
no	no	(NOH)

Glossary

alpaca (al-PAK-uh)—a South American animal that is related to the llama

empire (EM-pire)—a large territory ruled by a powerful leader

executive branch (eg-ZEK-yoo-tiv BRANCH)—the part of government that makes sure laws are followed

export (EK-sport)—to send and sell goods to other countries

guano (GWAH-noh)—dried bird or bat droppings, used as fertilizer

independent (in-di-PEN-duhnt)—free from the control of other people or things

industry (IN-duh-stree)—a single branch of business or trade

judicial branch (joo-DISH-uhl BRANCH)—the part of government that explains laws

legislative branch (LEJ-iss-lay-tiv BRANCH)—the part of government that passes bills that become laws

matador (MA-tah-dor)—a bullfighter

reed (REED)—a tall plant with hollow stems that grows in wetlands

Internet Sites

FactHound offers a safe, fun way to find Internet sites related to this book. All of the sites on FactHound have been researched by our staff.

Here's how:
1. Visit *www.facthound.com*
2. Type in this special code **0736837582** for age-appropriate sites. Or enter a search word related to this book for a more general search.
3. Click on the **Fetch It** button.

FactHound will fetch the best sites for you!

Read More

Italia, Bob. *Peru.* The Countries. Edina, Minn.: Abdo, 2002.

Knox, Barbara. *Peru.* Many Cultures, One World. Mankato, Minn.: Blue Earth Books, 2004.

O'Sullivan, MaryCate. *Peru.* Faces and Places. Chanhassen, Minn.: Child's World, 2001.

Yip, Dora, and Janet Heisey. *Welcome to Peru.* Welcome to My Country. Milwaukee: Gareth Stevens, 2002.

Index